Sino-Nigerian Developmental Relations and Issues

Sino-Nigerian Developmental Relations and Issues

Abhirup Bhunia

ATLANTIC

PUBLISHERS & DISTRIBUTORS (P) LTD

Published by
ATLANTIC
PUBLISHERS & DISTRIBUTORS (P) LTD
7/22, Ansari Road, Darya Ganj, New Delhi-110002
Phones : +91-11-40775252, 40775214, 23273880, 23275880
Fax: +91-11-23285873
Web: www.atlanticbooks.com
E-mail: orders@atlanticbooks.com

Printed & bound in India by Atlantic Print Services

Dedicated to well-wishers

Preface

The bilateral relations between the Federal Republic of Nigeria and the People's Republic of China have expanded on growing bilateral trade and strategic cooperation. The relations between these two countries which started formally in 1971 have grown, especially when Nigeria has become an important source of oil and petroleum for China's rapidly-growing economy, and Nigeria is receiving extensive economic, military and political support from China. Nigerian government has developed close military cooperation with China, which has supplied arms, equipment, training and technology to the Nigerian armed forces to fight insurgents in the oil-rich Niger Delta and to protect Nigeria's oil resources.

China also helped develop and launch the Nigerian communications satellite (NigComSat-1) in 2007 to expand cellular and Internet networks in Central Africa.

Apart from expansion of trade, both nations agreed to a four-point plan a few years ago to improve bilateral relations, a key component of which was to expand trade and investments in agriculture, telecommunications, energy and infrastructure development. Furthermore, China agreed to buy a controlling stake in the Kaduna oil refinery that would produce 110,000 barrels per day (17,000 m3/d). Nigeria also promised to give preference to Chinese oil firms for contracts for oil exploration in the Niger Delta and Chad Basin. In 2006, China also agreed to grant a loan of USD 1 billion to Nigeria to help upgrade and modernize its railway networks. In 2005, Nigeria agreed to supply PetroChina with 30,000 barrels per day (4,800 m3/d) of oil for USD 800 million.

However, there have been certain issues in this partnership for development. There has been an alleged 'flooding' of

Nigerian markets with cheap Chinese goods, which has become a sensitive political issue. Combined with the importation of second-hand European products, it has adversely affected Nigeria's domestic industries, especially textiles, and has led to the closure of over 50 textile mills and the laying-off of a large number of textile workers during last one decade. As a reaction, the Nigerian militants have threatened to attack Chinese workers and projects in Niger Delta. Academics have therein placed blame on FDI and the neoliberal globalisation regime in order, rather ideologically.

Unemployment is also increasing in Nigeria. From 13.4% in 2004, it rose to 21.1% in 2010. The rise in redundancy cannot be entirely attributed to global recession of 2007-08, and its aftereffects. When Chinese MNCs start business in Nigeria, the host state fails to take employment advantage of FDI owing to lack of a qualified workforce. When Chinese FDI was growing steadily, employment in Nigeria was either stagnant or declining, partly because China was sending along its human resources to Nigeria instead of employing local people. However, they are not cheap labour which China is known for, but men in senior positions doing skilled job. Poor educational standards in Nigeria hardly offered any labour force good enough for such positions. A major issue therefore is that investments in Nigeria should lead to job creation, development and improvement in the living standards of labour, which it does not—the reason being a failed state, I argue.

Some experts have alleged that China-Nigeria economic relationship is exploitive. While Nigeria is exporting primary goods, its imports are value-added products. It has led to de-industrialization in Nigeria, retarding its development. China can no longer be treated as a poor country as it is today capable of same exploitation as the Western countries. It is in effect no different from the imperialists. Some perceive China as perpetuating Western neoliberal hegemony because the investments of Chinese companies in Africa are largely driven by the basic aim of seeking oil for the production in China of manufactured goods by Chinese firms working as subcontractors for big Western corporations, with the bulk of the profit accruing to the latter. All of these arguments fail to take into account the role the host state plays in making or breaking its chances to exploit FDI for its own good.

Nigerian people continue to reel under poverty while China's FDI in that country is increasing. But FDI in developing countries can be beneficial only if the host country ensures that it works to its benefit. Thus, Nigeria needs to develop its productive sectors to lift its masses out of poverty. It must be said herein that there is substantial scope for sector-specific and region-specific analyses and explanations, given that the mandate in this book doesn't cover the same.

The book is substantially based on research carried out at the University of Sussex, UK. It studies Sino-Nigerian development relations and brings to light certain important issues that need to be addressed, especially by Nigeria which has been unable to develop its industry, reduce poverty and unemployment, despite increase in trade between these two countries, and inward FDI.

The approach of the book is concise and analytical to give focused attention to the issues at hand. It is an academic product and thus makes reference to several and diverse studies. The book will be useful for students/scholars/researchers of political economy, development policy, politics, economics and even the general audience with an interest in the field.

As far as acknowledgments go, I take this opportunity to thank my professors/lecturers in University of Sussex for furthering my understanding of the field and contributing immensely to all intellectual exercises that I undertook during my time there. Just for the record, some additions to the book were done during my time as a senior research analyst at the Institute of Economic Growth, New Delhi.

I find this an appropriate place to extend my deep sense of gratitude to my family and other dear ones simply for being there at all times.

Abhirup Bhunia

List of Abbreviations

FDI	:	Foreign Direct Investment
GDP	:	Gross Domestic Product
GCC	:	Global Commodity Chain
HDI	:	Human Development Index
ISI	:	Import Substitution Industrialisation
LDC	:	Least Developed Country(s)
MAN	:	Manufacturers Association of Nigeria
MNC	:	Multinational Corporation
NBS	:	National Bureau of Statistics, Nigeria
NFDC	:	Nigerian Foreign Development Council
NIE	:	New Institutional Economics
OECD	:	Organisation of Economic Cooperation and Development
TNC	:	Transnational Corporation
UNDP	:	United Nations Development Programme
WST	:	World Systems Theory

Graphs and Tables

Contents

1
Introduction

Nigeria clocked an impressive average annual GDP growth rate of 7% from 2004 to 2009 (AfDB, 2009). Growth has over the last eight years been sustained at a decent level. This was also the time when Nigeria opened itself up to greater capital inflows. Since then Chinese investors have steadily pumped billions into the country even as Nigeria has risen in prominence to become the second-biggest destination for Chinese outward Foreign Direct Investment (FDI). Over time, trade between the two countries has expanded rapidly too and touched $18bn in 2012 (OECD, 2011). As mineral rents continue to accrue to Nigeria and investment flows from China go on unabated, the Sino-Nigerian relationship has only deepened. Sadly however, wealth creation and accumulation at one end of the pole in Nigeria has only been accompanied by a lack of development at the other. Extreme poverty and chronic unemployment continue to characterize Nigeria's underdevelopment story—at a time when Africa is pursuing a neoliberal agenda with conviction. Ever since, some scholars have debated on the possibility of Chinese neoimperialism in Africa, while others argue that it is a developmental pact for good.

The growing relationship has received much interest in policy and academic circles, while generally the China-Africa relationship continues to be of interest to academia the world over. I argue that much scholarship that portrays neoliberal globalisation running over sovereign territories particularly in sub-Saharan Africa assumes institutional supremacy of global markets and undermines the state as a means to, and an architect of, development. The analysis in this book not only puts the state at the forefront of analysis but also lays bare the absurd trickledown theory of neoliberalism represented by a self-determining market and a non-interventionist state. I seek to bring together and build on different elements of statism and add new elements to it while not adhering to any given blueprint, as I believe there can be none.

While "...structuralists conceive foreign trade as a 'zero-sum game' enabling the rich advanced countries to prosper at the expense of the poor backward ones" (Lall, 2000: 67), neoliberals never miss a chance to trumpet free trade and FDI as harbingers of development in poor countries. Ficker (2005) rightly seeks an end to such mutually exclusive and confrontational portrayals. In a rejection of what we know as the neo-classical economic theory, what is instead required is a more nuanced approach to development wherein one needs to reject the dubious claims of neo-classical economists for whom the market is an universal remedy, while not sharing the dim view of structuralists and dependency theorists for whom the existing world system in its current form does not provide any real hope for development in the poor countries.

Such a synthesis might appear to be consistent with the broader themes of new institutional economics (NIE) or statism per se. While their features might indeed overlap, the issue to my mind is more concrete. The question really is how wise institutional support and state supervision can *manage* capitalism in a manner in which developing countries, and the labour force within, stand to benefit. The broad theoretical contours of NIE have to do with 'bringing the state back'. But it's not just that. As Hariss et al. (1995: 1) put it, "... NIE does not simply reintroduce the state...rather it shows that neither state nor market is *invariably* the best way in which to organise the provision of goods and services" (*ibid.*: 1, emphasis added). The NIE critique of neo-classical economics simply rests on the idea that what is required is not an overt reliance on market forces but a combination of a (strong) state and the market. It also attempts to embed the market in the social context. But unlike earlier critiques of neo-classical economics, NIE does not seek to overturn markets, but obviously with its thrust on state intervention rejects the concept of a 'self-regulated market' like the original institutionalist, Karl Polanyi did. While not very different from NIE as far as fundamentals are concerned, the neo-Listian political economy framework has a dedicated focus on the state's role in development.

In this paper, I will conduct a critical study of the Nigerian state in the context of rising Chinese FDI in Nigeria—which should be perceived as part of a wider neoliberal wave in Africa. And it is only fair that I point out that my choosing to focus on Chinese FDI has only to do with the fact that it carries much topical credence. While steering clear of engaging in a discussion that necessarily invokes a pro/anti-markets tussle, this paper sets out to (a) document how the neoliberal policies of free trade and FDI haven't had their benefits on the Nigerian people while wealth has continued to accumulate at the top and (b) account for this underdevelopment in the context of rising Chinese FDI by making the host state (Nigeria) the focal point of analysis. At this juncture, it is worth stating that choosing to focus on Nigeria rather than dealing with China-Africa relations in general makes the study more specific. At the same time, as one of the largest economies in Africa, a study of the Nigerian state will provide invaluable insights into and add to the existing literature on the state.

Given that this dissertation substantially concerns itself with FDI as such, it is worth quoting here the convincing words of Ha-Joon Chang on transnational capital:

> ...The current literature tends to regard the process of globalisation and the rise of TNCs as an unstoppable process that no one can control, in which nations, specially developing nations, are passive agents that will have to fully embrace the process or perish. However, such a view is misleading since there is a lot of room for manoeuvre by national governments.... (Chang, 1998: 113)

It is this portrayal of passivity of states that I will challenge by arguing that an LDC like Nigeria, although constrained by the existing world order to an extent, is very well capable of bargaining for better terms of FDI and if proper policies are taken to "intelligently use TNCs for their long term developmental purposes" (Chang, *ibid.*), then the need to fall back on the world-system as a justification for Nigerian underdevelopment might not be necessary after all. What follows is not just arguing that state agency is intact in the face of globalisation, but also highlighting the internal explanations for such underdevelopment that are overlooked in the mad rush to project China as an evil imperial agent bent upon destroying Africa—in this case Nigeria.

The paper is divided into four sections: The first section will be a comprehensive review of the existing literature on the subject, not only dealing with the specific case of Chinese economic relationship with Nigeria, but also on broader debates to do with FDI/free trade, the state and development, thus providing for a theoretical context. Thereafter, I will be talking about the Nigerian state in detail. This chapter will be further divided into three sections where I deal with FDI, international trade, and the aspect of neo-colonialism one after the other, following which I will compile my arguments into a summary and conclude.

2

Ongoing Debates: A Literature Review

The 53 year old post-colonial state of Nigeria has experienced a political roller-coaster ride, from a parliamentary form of government to a presidential one and from phases of dictatorships to civilian democracy. As far as economic regime goes, everything from protectionism and economic nationalism to semi-openness to full-fledged neoliberalism has had its share of reign. A broad spectrum of scholarship on Nigeria deals with the diverse aspects of the state: the rentier state, corruption, neoliberalism, social fragmentation, economic and social development, etc. Nigeria's recent camaraderie with China has gained much global attention and one notices some interesting additions to the literature. Today Nigeria is often cited as an example of neoliberalism at its worst, wherein the political elite display disquieting wealth, while the masses continue to reel under poverty. The debate surrounding this, as one would expect, is dotted with a plethora of views on both sides of the spectrum.

True to his Marxist lineage, Beckman (2007) makes class the focal point of his discussion on the Nigerian state and argues that the state's role in the ongoing capitalist development in Nigeria is one of 'comprador', a collaborator for capital. He goes on to say that the state comes across as an agent of imperialism by acting as an organ of furthering the penetration of foreign capital in the country. He sees the state quite simply as enabling capitalist accumulation both foreign and indigenous, and in so far as FDI is specifically concerned, seems to suggest the existence of a transnational imperialistic arrangement that exploits the masses. But importantly he makes the point, and rightly so, that while the state has indeed been promoting capitalist development, it has done a shoddy job of it. In other words, neoliberal capitalism has not had the desired outcomes in terms of development of the masses. But then, his rejection of the idea that state power can be used to steer national capitalist development and calling the idea simplistic, is one significant point of departure as far as the argument in this book goes.

Turner (2007) trains his guns on corruption and links it with the ongoing capitalist accumulation in Nigeria while suggesting a triangular relationship between the state, the domestic capitalists and foreign capital that facilitates diversion of resources on a grand scale. According to him, middlemen are a key to the formation of an illicit informal system wherein foreign capital does not take the logical route to entry:

> A foreign businessman is successful in Nigeria not because he offers a competitive price, high quality produce, efficient service, or the commodity which best suits local needs.... A businessman is successful because he has made contact with the right middleman and gets access to the right government official who finds the foreign firms' proposal attractive. (Turner, 2007: 67)

Alleging that the China-Nigeria economic relationship is one that is exploitative, Sanusi (2013) points to the declining terms of trade faced by Nigeria as it imports mostly value added goods while exporting primary products for the most parts. Consequently, this leads to de-industrialisation in Nigeria thus disabling development. This argument fits well into the well established standpoint of dependency theorists. However, *technically* China and Nigeria don't fit into the core-periphery formation, as China is more of a semi-periphery in world-systems terminology. However, Sanusi makes it clear that China can no longer be treated as a poor country as it is today 'a giant' capable of the *same* exploitation as the Western countries. In fact, Maswana (2007) resolves this issue authoritatively. He concludes that the China-Africa link despite being a South-South relationship fundamentally reveals characteristics of the usual core-periphery relationship although China is short of being classified as a 'core' economy. The South-South developmental relationship between China and Nigeria, and more broadly Africa, has often been on a normative plank signposted as a counter to the Western neoliberal world order. Arrighi (2007) makes this point, while others like Sanusi think China is no different from Western imperialists. Some perceive China to be perpetuating Western neoliberal hegemony by simply affixing itself to a global commodity chain in which surplus profits all but accrue to Western MNCs:

> Chinese-owned companies' investments in Africa are largely driven by a basic agenda of seeking fuel and minerals inputs for the production in China of manufactures by Chinese firms working as subcontractors for big Western corporations, with the bulk of the profits going to the latter. (Cheng, 2007: para. 20)

Ogen (2008) paints a rather disastrous picture of the Nigerian economy which is indeed the right picture to paint if one were to go by both empirical data and realities on the ground. While addressing the contemporary Sino-Nigerian trade relations and Chinese investments in Nigeria "within the purview of the undercurrents of neo-liberalism," the author notes that China is not only exploiting Nigeria's natural resources to further its strategic needs, but also through its investments de-industrialising important sectors of the Nigerian economy. He further notes that indigenous enterprise in the country is stifled even as infant industries are getting smashed up owing to Chinese imports that are cheaper. Ogen rests his argument on two logics. One, that the political economy of natural resources, with its exploitative underpinnings, has played itself out in Nigeria thanks to Chinese FDI in the sector. Secondly, he thinks that the idea of Nigerian development would benefit greatly from import substitution industrialisation (ISI) and not liberalisation. Underdevelopment, by such accounts, is reproduced and sustained through incorporating Nigeria into the global capitalist economy as a peripheral appendage.

With respect to Chinese FDI in the African oil sector, Oliveira (2008) breaks away from Olga's views by debunking the premise that China is being 'hyper-exploitative', and instead suggests that the political economy of oil has historically not been particularly benign. There is no newness therefore in the China-Africa link that should command such negative exposure. He refers to the perennially non-developmental nature of resource-seeking FDI while Mehlum et al. (2004) have sought to rise above such pessimism by laying down certain institutional principles necessary in resource-rich countries to bring the best out. The authors classify institutions as 'grabber-friendly' and 'producer-friendly' in which the latter category defies Oliveira's non-developmentalism argument. It follows that if the institutional setting is right, entrepreneurs will be drawn towards the productive sectors of the economy, eventually leading to overall economic development. In the aforementioned analysis, Mehlum et al. situate Nigeria in the 'grabber-friendly' category. But there is also great potential for development led by resource sector FDI. And this, according to Robinson et al. (2006), can greatly be realised if rents do not automatically lead to political patronage. In the subsequent chapter on the Nigerian state, I will deal more fully with the political structure of the state, including discussing neopatrimonialism. The resource curse hypothesis is anyways challenged in a recent study by Meyersson, et al. (2008) which provides novel empirical data to suggest that the characteristics of the trading partner significantly influence the nature of trade in Africa and there is no universal form of exploitative trade relation. The authors point out that Africa's trade with China in comparison to US or India for instance actually turns out to be beneficial to Africa. However, whereas exporting to China leads to an increase in GDP, at least part of which is being directed to the government, the state "in turn is not spending it on the people" (*ibid.*: 18).

Since the question being probed is that of Nigerian development (social justice being an inevitable part of it) and not merely accumulation of wealth, which in any case Nigeria has managed to do fairly well, part of the answer lies in effective management of natural assets for the benefit of the masses by bringing about social welfare, human development and protection of human rights. For Collier (2010), the 'social value' of natural resources is a function of the political system and "the better is the system, the more able is the society to harness the potential value of its natural assets" (*ibid.*: 1106). He argues that improving the management of natural resources in existing weak political systems (like say, Nigeria) should go hand in hand with the more long-term goal of ensuring that natural assets don't cause damage to the political system in the first place as the two are complimentary. Furthering his proposition, the author in a recent conference on governance said that African countries should be able to transform their natural resources into prosperity.

But a divergent set of arguments running through the literature actually portrays the Chinese embrace of Africa as neo-colonialist. And while this happens, the African state gets more and more drawn into an exploitative relationship with the 'predatory capitalist' that China is. This line of argument rests on the belief that the state as a preconceived category, a historical entity that overrides social classes, is shaky under globalism and that transnationalisation sets crippling limits to the Third World—particularly African—state (Amin, 1990: 75). More generally, multinationals working in developing countries are seen as blocking development in the host country rather than aiding it and in fact contributing to domestic inequality along with denationalising, and even de-industrialising, the host economy (Frank, 1972).

Junbo warns of the possibility that Chinese FDI might lead to exploitation of local labour and result in environmental degradation due to excessive natural resource extraction. The predictive nature of his argument does not take away from the logic underlying the statement though. Exploitation of labour by FDI is a well-documented aspect of the literature and Junbo warns Nigeria's time under Chinese FDI can end up being a new addition to a whole host of such instances. Many scholars suggest that the labour-capital dichotomy and the divergence between the two classes therein is sought to be further expanded in the face of rising FDI in LDCs and developing countries. Roychowdhury (2004) for instance talks about labour's "declining political leverage" as a result of rising FDI in poor countries.

Deploying a general theory of FDI and blending it with the Nigerian case, Ayanwale (2007) on the other hand argues that FDI has in fact translated into economic development in

Nigeria. He particularly mentions FDI in the communication sector has having potential for enabling large-scale development, while pausing to caution that FDI has not had any significant positive effect on human capital. His study is of a fairly recent vintage and therefore by design generously includes FDI by Chinese MNCs. But Dutse, et al. (2011) guard against taking technology spillovers for granted and urges for an active policy framework which encourages FDI and tie-ups with foreign companies on selected manufacturing technologies that will strengthen the technological capabilities of indigenous firms in Nigeria. Spillovers are in any case a debatable aspect of FDI's impacts on developing countries. Even the aspect of wage spillover—meaning that local firms are likely to raise wages in response to foreign companies paying higher wages, thus raising general wage level—is also subject to scrutiny. However in sum, a general wage level rise as a result of FDI is confirmed by empirical studies conducted by Lipsey. Studies also show that FDI provides an impetus to domestic investments, a lack of which contributes to economic slowdown. And this has been somewhat true for Chinese FDI in Nigeria too, since Nigerian businessmen have learned to export productively by using Chinese models and have profited by partnering in joint ventures with the Chinese (Nabine, 2009).

Haroz (2011) while conceding a range of benefits accruing to Nigeria from Chinese FDI including new jobs being created through investments in manufacturing and construction, feels it is important to note that "...African producers and workers may strain under the weight of foreign competition" (*ibid.*: 77). Trade between China and Nigeria is in fact a subject of much debate and many scholars have drawn attention to the deleterious effects of rising trade with China. Ayittey is one of them. He tracks the manufacturing sector in Nigeria and submits that the influx of Chinese products has destroyed the textiles industry in Kano, one of Nigeria's bigger cities. He reveals that the number of factories churning out textile products numbered 500 in the eighties and this number has gone down to fewer than 100 today, most operating below full capacity. Akinrinade too while conceding some positive effects of what he calls "South-South neoliberalism" sticks to the Nigerian textile sector and argues for quotas to protect the textile industry. For him, like Ayittey, protectionism is the way forward if development of the Nigerian masses is the desired goal. Many scholars however refute the anti-FDI stance and argue that there is merit in advancing with a judicious mix of both indigenous and foreign capital/knowledge while appreciating the reciprocal relationship between the two (Borensztein, et al. 1998).

3

FDI, Host State and Mal-development: The Sino-Nigerian Story

Before diving into the Nigerian case, I think it is pertinent to understand the position in a general context. A very concise global discussion on how FDI can be tied to development in the host state through policy precision in the latter follows.[1]

When we talk of development, what we are essentially driving at is whether the living standards of people have improved. And in the context of FDI, this largely translates into the question of how the labour force has fared in the face of internationalisation of capital, in other words the inflow of large scale foreign investments. Globalisation is said to have changed the very nature of labour, a key factor of production that has its own set of dimensions and dynamics. Over the decades globalisation has undergone multiple transmutations. Moving beyond just international trade, it is cross-border capital flows that have come to dominate the dialogue on globalism. Indeed, globalisation today has less to do with simple imports and exports than it has to do with foreign direct investment (FDI) and the internationalisation

1. This part draws heavily from my essay 'Labour in times of rising foreign direct investment in developing countries' published in Open Democracy under the Digital Commons.

of production. FDI as a stock of worldwide GDP has risen tremendously over the decades. For the year ending 2011, worldwide FDI was recorded at a massive $20.4 trillion. There has been an immense rise in FDI flowing in to developing countries in recent times. About 50% of global FDI in 2012 was targeted at China alone (UNCTAD, 2012), with India and Brazil among the other investment hotspots.

Since FDI has strong implications for labour, it has become a political imperative for governments to engage with it. States have so far reacted to FDI in different ways. The instances of FDI being repelled are dwarfed by the many times countries have competed among themselves to attract FDI. In a bid to do so, changes to labour regulations—in most cases, a relaxation of rules—have ensued. There are examples where host countries have benefited in terms of employment as multinational corporations (MNCs) not only pay higher wages, but they also ensure better working conditions. There is also plenty of evidence to the contrary; indeed, in some cases the empirical evidence shows that MNCs do not have high wage standards. More fundamentally, FDI brings in enormous changes to the local economy.

While some view FDI as entirely anti-labour, a slightly more sophisticated perspective is that benefits to labour in the host country are often tilted in favour of skilled workers. Amidst the cacophony of firms strategising investments based on what is profitable, and the resultant rise of what is known as the 'competition state,' the position of labour has undergone significant changes. Advocates of neo-liberalism seem to be in favour of FDI. Others see merit in FDI that is calibrated and qualified to protect the interests of labour. For many others, the very nature of FDI is a political project to protect the interests of capital.

The dialogue can no longer, however, be merely reduced to a confrontation between capital and labour. Too often, proponents of the anti-globalisation school simply identify multinational corporations as the chief beneficiaries of globalisation (automatically implying that the working classes have not benefited). From this perspective, the issue is a conflict between capital and labour. Various oppositions to foreign capital, rooted in different ideologies, are oftentimes grouped under the single umbrella of anti-globalisation. The anathema to FDI is often vague, generalised and fails to take into account the environment, the institutions and the uniqueness of each case. The relatively underprivileged state of labour is, in fact, not so much a corollary of FDI as it is a condition created by the state, mistakenly hoping to encourage FDI even as it keeps engaging in unconstructive competition. It should be acknowledged that the disadvantaged position of labour is seen as going hand in hand with the rise in FDI. This situation, attributable to a "race to the bottom" initiated by states, is anchored in the misleading notion that transnational capital inevitably embraces cheap labour.

An unshakably negative view of capital does not take into account the constructive role that FDI plays in the labour markets of developing countries. FDI has in some cases played an instrumental role in transforming countries from being exporters of raw materials (a 'periphery country' characteristic) to exporters of manufactures, sometimes even relatively high-tech ones (Lipsey, 2004). In these cases, FDI has actually helped labour move up the ladder, with skills imparted and technology diffused without any additional institutional capacity building by the state during that time. The question to ask is not which of the two—labour or capital—benefits from FDI, but what are the circumstances under which labour can extract benefits from foreign capital in developing countries? While the profit motive of capital is too naive not to be acknowledged, FDI in fact should not be seen as necessarily anti-labour. Despite the view that FDI is class biased, FDI wages in fact have a significant skill premium attached to it, meaning that those that have the required skills receive higher wages. In developing countries that are commanding greater FDI by the day, these skills do not get equally or universally imparted, with the result that a level-playing field is being denied at the very outset. In such cases, the much criticized, rich-poor divide is only widened by foreign capital. To stem the negative impacts of FDI, states can step in by not only offering free lunches, as it were, but through the long-term strengthening of its institutional environment. "In principle, under the right institutional circumstances, countries or regions could exert bargaining power over MNCs, and regulate them in such a way as to generate significant benefits for their communities" (Braunstein and Epstein, 2002).

First, it is important to establish that FDI is not simply a single-minded hunt for low wages. A cursory look at the existing data shows that the cost of labour is seldom the decisive element in FDI decisions. The Philippines received \$917mn in FDI in the first half of 2012, whereas FDI of \$5.8bn was pumped into Brazil in June 2012 alone, a BRIC country and one of the fastest growing economies in the world. The price of labour in Philippines and Brazil are \$2.01 and \$11.65 per hour, respectively. As noted, even though labour costs in Brazil are more than five times that of the Philippines, the South American country has been much more attractive to foreign investors. The lack of FDI in the Philippines, a low-wage country, is explained by the fact that foreign investors are no longer principally concerned with utilising investment locations as platforms for cheap labour from which to export inexpensive manufactures to the affluent markets of the North (Amerasinghe & Modesto, 2012). Brazil's internal market growth is one of the reasons why FDI is attracted to that country. India, with its massive population, receives a fair share of FDI for its exceptionally large market size.

In addition, since FDI seeks relatively skilled labour, and the benefits of FDI accrue to those with a certain degree of educational background, education is a definite policy imperative for developing states. FDI has a direct negative effect on "less-schooled" workers (Rama, 2002). FDI, therefore, seems to offer a definite 'return on education.' FDI has also tended to focus on sectors that have more to do with the use of the brain. For example, in developing countries FDI has largely been in sectors like information technology, the services sector, hospitality business and so on, with the exception of the natural resources sector (solely ascribable to a region's natural endowments). In China, manufacturing has had the lion's share of FDI, but one must simultaneously note that the percentage of low skilled and unskilled jobs in manufacturing declined by 29% since the 1970s even as knowledge-intensive jobs (those commanding understanding of math, computer and science) have gone up and are predicted to continue to rise.

Foreign owned companies have offered higher salaries to managers, engineers and the like to retain them. The benefits of FDI have not seeped into the broader labour market where there are low literacy levels and high unemployment. That foreign owned firms tend to hire more educated and better qualified workers also partly explains why FDI wages are higher than domestic wages. In India, for instance, according to separate reports by McKinsey, the Confederation of Indian Industry and the Boston Consulting Group, most of India's 1.2 billion young people are unemployable because they lack the necessary skills required to service a rapidly changing global market. Because of a crumbling educational infrastructure, these youth have not been taught the necessary skills. As OECD noted, "a level of technological, educational and infrastructure achievement in a developing country does, other things being equal, equip it better to benefit from a foreign presence in its markets."

The disadvantageous position of labour in developing countries can thus be attributable in part to a deficient educational structure and an inefficient institutional setting, both domestic factors, rather than the mere presence of foreign capital. The quality of labour, therefore, is what states should focus on and use as an asset to attract FDI rather than offering cheap labour or fiscally unsound lower taxes as incentives to foreign capital. Any developing country resources should create efficient educational and vocational programmes and useful public bureaucracies to draw in foreign capital. It is therefore the policy context within which FDI occurs that determines whether it is going to work to the benefit of the developing countries or to its detriment.

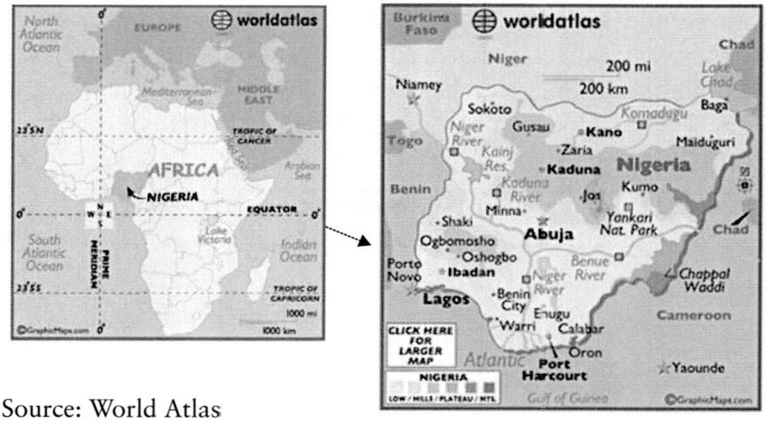

Source: World Atlas
http://www.worldatlas.com

In the aftermath of Nigerian independence (1 Oct, 1960), the civilian government broadly embarked on an 'open economy' expedition where foreign capital was welcome, although it played a limited role then. Primary commodities export was emphasised and domestic entrepreneurship somewhat encouraged. Close on the heels of the oil boom, the state undertook a massive indigenisation decree. Later, a second indigenisation decree followed—this was to be in 1977. The idea then in Nigeria—as in Africa—was to wrench *control* of the economy from foreign hands. Economic policymaking was confined to nationalisation of private companies and wresting state control of the economy. This was in line with more widespread nationalistic policies gaining ground on a global scale, from Asia to Africa to Latin America. A neoliberal counteroffensive that was gradually taking shape and took a fuller form in the nineties saw the world revel in the glorification of global markets even as developing countries, including sub-Saharan Africa, gradually liberalised their economies. Today, Nigeria is running at full throttle neoliberal pace.

And it is in the context of Nigeria's run under the aegis of neoliberal policymaking that Chinese FDI and trade must be looked into, and not as a separate occurrence of its own that should warrant incredulity and awe. The figure below, by the way, indicates that trade volumes of Nigeria have very firmly gone up over the last decade and a half, except a blip in 2008-09, which was in line with global trends during the 2008 financial crisis.

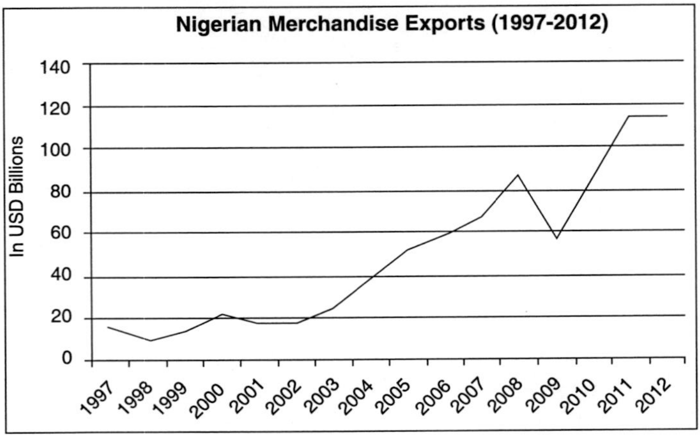

Source: World Development Indicators, various issues, World Bank.

Contrary to popular belief, Chinese investment in Nigeria is not limited to the resources sector. However, although FDI is being pumped into the manufacturing, communications, financial and agro-business sectors, natural resources command a significant share of FDI. Nigeria suffers from not just capital deficit but serious infrastructural bottlenecks. Thus, the lack of capital has only justified the hunt for foreign investors. And Chinese capital's pursuance of natural resources in Nigeria is hardly unusual. As Daniel (1991: para 8) puts it, "[Since] mineral deposits, forests and fisheries do not move to world financial centres, companies must move to them."

But with Nigerian Human Development Index (HDI) ranking as low as 153 out of a total of 186 countries (UNDP), even lower than the sub-Saharan African average HDI, there is little to celebrate as far as development is concerned. The following figure shows the pace of development relative to FDI inflows in which I employ widely-available HDI figures to indicate development and map it against the inflow of FDI in the respective years. It is interesting to note that FDI inflows into Nigeria have steadily increased even during a time of global financial crisis, demonstrating its significance.

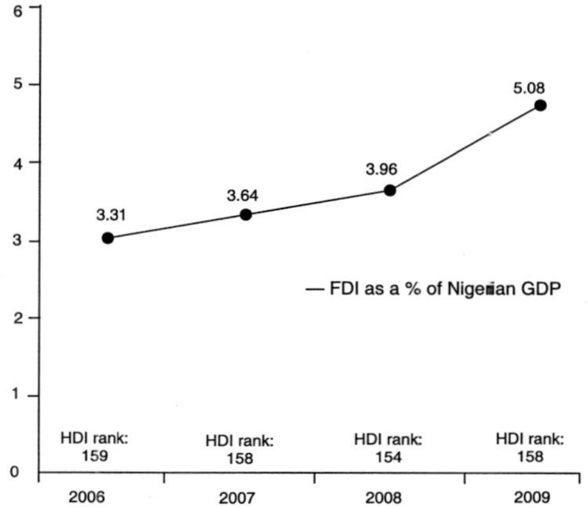

Fig. 1: Nigeria under Neoliberalism: Development vis-a-vis foreign Capital

Nigeria has seen a steady rise of FDI since early 2000s whereas its HDI rank has not improved as it continues to rank in the unflattering range of roughly 155-160 in a list of about 187 countries. *Source*: World Bank, UNDP

As the figure confirms, opening up the economy and pursuing a neoliberal agenda has at best been futile and detrimental at worst. But the persistence, if not exacerbation, of poverty and inequality in the region has resulted in the rise of a discourse that is dominated by talk of exploitation by foreign capital, mal-effects of free trade, the injustices of the world-system, and so on.

While not purely dogmatic, these explanations seem to not just overlook the internal explanation for underdevelopment, but also preclude the use of state power as a very real means to development. By assuming that the state is incapable of managing capitalist globalisation to benefit their own people, African states are being robbed of their agency in the face of rapid globalisation. Glyn (2005) makes the point that there is a tendency to exaggerate the effects of internationalisation. Regardless of the degree to which a state is integrated into the global economy, there are very real domestic problems that hinder egalitarian policymaking, which are fundamental while external influences are merely additional (*ibid.*: 408). In fact, there is a need to "reinsert African agency into China-Africa relations" as most analyses of China's topical involvement in Africa needlessly catapult China into the driving seat (Mohan and Lampert, 2013). Thus, placing African politics at the heart of any understanding of China-Africa relations is crucial (*ibid.*). Accordingly, FDI is unlikely to be harmful to a LDC without the state being a reckless party to it, implicitly or otherwise.

It might be argued that Nigeria not only failed its own agency by failing to attract FDI in the productive sectors of the economy, but also never managed to extract the benefits out of Chinese resource seeking FDI. Instead what it has done is put in place a distorted policy of attracting FDI mindlessly without tying it to the developmental needs of the country. For instance its policy of incentivising resource

FDI by not only allowing 100% repatriation of capital but smugly offering generous "tax holidays" to such investments from TNCs (Nigerian Investment Promotion Council, 2012), in effect enables and sustains—or even sets off—the kind of "loot" that it has been alleged the Chinese are engaging in. Such tax benefits reduces the ability of a resource rich country like Nigeria to take advantage of soaring profits during a commodity boom like the one experienced in 2008, while windfall gains accrue to the foreign companies alone. In any case, tax holidays are hardly a determining factor as far as investment decisions are concerned. Not surprisingly, the rate of growth of FDI inflows into Nigeria has not risen substantially ever since the incentives were put in place, demonstrating its inappropriateness. Fowowe argues that the negative effects of fiscal incentives in Nigeria include not just a loss of revenue but also rent seeking and corruption. State policy at the moment in Nigeria is one where the rich are being indirectly subsidised even as social welfare remains woefully deficient.

According to Stiglitz (2012), Africa's resource could be a 'blessing' provided the right kinds of policy decisions are taken. For example, he suggests putting in place a windfall gains tax to ensure foreign companies don't manage to put away all profits when natural resources command greater price on world markets. What Nigeria has instead done is allowed companies engaged in mining of solid minerals to benefit from a tax holiday for the first three years of operation while the Mines and Minerals Act, 2007 allows this to be extended for a further two years. And, with its long history of unparalleled corruption, "well designed, competitive, [and] transparent auctions" of natural assets, as advocated by Stiglitz, are pretty much alien concepts in the state. In fact, but for the mind-boggling corruption of the political elites, financing infrastructural projects in Nigeria should not have been difficult given the immense natural resource based wealth the country boasts of. It is in this light that it must be noted that manufacturing in Nigeria constitutes a paltry 4% of its GDP (Manufacturers Association of Nigeria, 2012). The following table and figure represent the sectoral division of the Nigerian economy year-wise. I will deal with corruption in a separate section. Let us start with the aspect of the role of the host state vis-à-vis FDI.

Nigeria Economy Structure in the Past two Decades

Year	Agriculture value added as % of GDP	Industry value added as % of GDP	Services, etc. as % of GDP	GDP annual % growth
1991-2000	32.88	43.66	23.45905	1.881248
2001-05	38.40	38.75	22.85373	11.14607
2006	32.00	41.92	26.08437	8.210965
2007	32.71	40.65	26.63375	6.828398
2008	32.85	41.48	25.66711	6.270264
2009	37.05	34.21	28.74467	6.934416
2010	23.96	25.81	50.2235	7.839739
2011	22.80	27.85	49.35475	4.653337
2012	22.36	26.72	50.91353	6.745196

Nigerian Economy Break-up

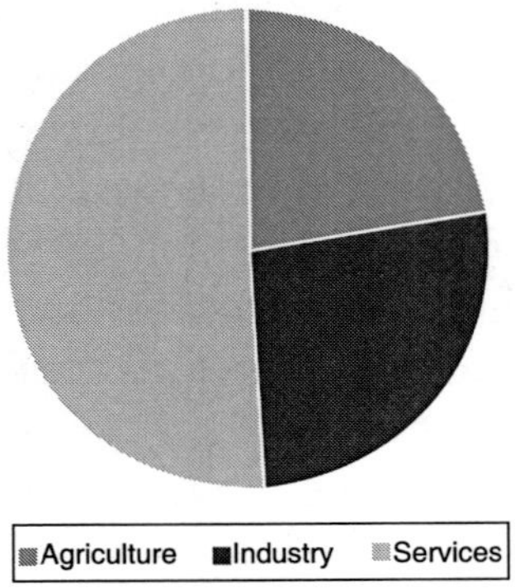

3.1 FDI and an Active State

The state's role in development is essentially two fold. One pertains largely to laying the foundation for sustainable growth by investing in social and physical infrastructure, and the second is to do with enabling development through proper utilisation of capital, including foreign capital. As Sen (2013) argues, it is only on a strong 'social foundation' that most economic successes in the history of mankind have come to pass. It is based on this social foundation, characterised by an 'educated, healthy labour force', that the bulk of the European industrial revolution and major Asian economic developments have taken place and the responsibility to lay this groundwork rests on the state (*ibid.*). Consequently, political authority which is territorially organised and delineated should be leveraged in achieving the pre-conditions for appropriate utilisation of capital that leads to development and social justice. Poulantzas had laid the foundation of nation-statism in political science with his observation as such that the "state is the heart of the exercise of political power" (Quoted in Palan, 1992: 23). Contemporary political-economy reading of this fundamental point made by Poulantzas can be found in development literature focused on the state. Famously, Amsden (1989) in her critique of the neo-classical ilk highlighted the role of the state in development in the developing countries. She was dealing with the South Korean state but the broader point she was driving at was that countries that have effectively put together independent stocks of 'knowledge' by state-interventions are more likely to do better in the globalised world. South Korea, for instance, was not merely content trying to reap the benefits of a Ricardian-styled comparative advantage in rice, and instead went on to subsidise innovation and value-added manufacturing. For Amsden, states need to supplement the market, not conform to them. In a comparative study of Nigeria and other developing economies, Kohli (2005) takes the Nigerian state to task and indicates that state-led developmentalism had utterly failed in Nigeria. And of the many mistakes he points out, the one that stands out is the charge that the state failed in training and organising a productive workforce. This harks back to Sen's point about the creation of a healthy workforce first.

Empirical studies also confirm that the benefits of FDI generally accrue to states with a relatively good quality workforce and hence state-sponsored education with the intention of creating a healthy workforce is a definite policy imperative (Graham, 2000; Rama, 2002; Al-Sadig, 2012). But sadly, since gaining independence Nigeria allocated an annual average of 5-8% of its total expenditure on education while other African countries, despite sharing the same historical realities with Nigeria, prioritised education with Ghana allocating 21%, Kenya 20% and Uganda 15% of their total expenditures to education (Adam and Olaniyi, 2003). The accompanying figure below in fact reflects the most recent available data on education expenditure in Nigeria.

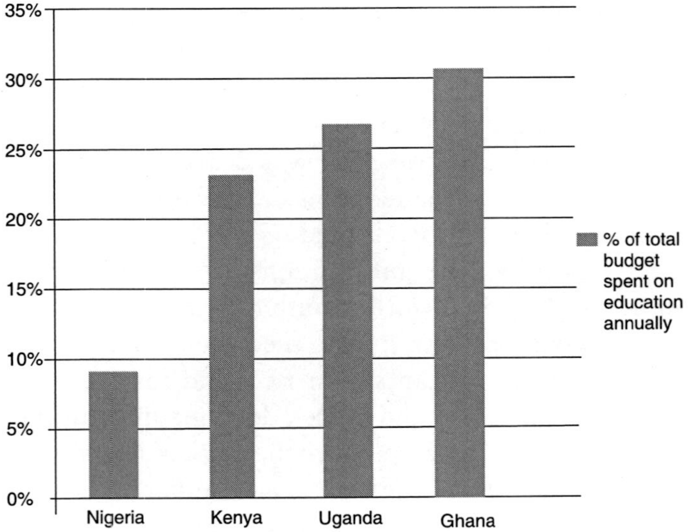

Fig. 2: Nigeria's allocation of a little less than 9% of its budget in 2013 for education stands in contrast to its peers in Africa, whose commitment to the creation of an educated human resource pool is way greater.

Source: Vanguard (Nigeria)

The results of a fresh study by Ozughalu and Ogwumike (2013) indicate that both in the short-run and long-run, economic growth, exports and foreign direct investment do not provide the way out of joblessness in Nigeria. But, the authors rightly contend that to surmount underdevelopment "...adequate mechanism should be put in place to ensure that economic growth, foreign direct investment and exports bring about optimum employment generation" (*ibid.*: 36). This 'adequate mechanism' includes state expenditure on quality education to reap what Rama (2002) calls FDI's 'return on education'. A table that follows indicates deteriorating primary school education enrolment in Nigeria, to not speak of higher and vocational education.

School Enrolment Ratio in Nigeria

Year	Enrolment Ratio
2006	114.4897
2007	111.6898
2008	109.2659
2009	102.0841
2010	88.90524
2011	92.45728
2012	89.29981

Source: WDI

Note: The enrolment ratio can go beyond 100 because of grade repetition or entry to school at ages younger/older than the typical age level for that grade. Data is only available for the given years.

When Chinese MNCs flock to Nigeria, the host state fails to take the employment advantages of FDI due to the lack of a qualified workforce. At a time when Chinese FDI was growing steadily, employment in Nigeria was either stagnant or declining, partly because China was exporting its human resources to Nigeria rather than employing locals. However, this is not to do with cheap labour costs (as China is usually known for). A study by Jauch (2011) reveals that most Chinese employees that are being brought to Nigeria are in executive positions, i.e. they are skilled jobs. Had educational standards in Nigeria been up to the mark and the labourforce good enough to be picked from, China would not have felt the need to expatriate its own citizens because by no measure is that cheaper than employing local Nigerians. The China-Nigeria economic relationship needs to be shaped in a manner in which investments result in job creation and development. On the contrary, in what Anele (2013) describes as "anti-people and anti-poor" policies, the concerns of the Nigerian labourforce are being carelessly overlooked simply to synthetically pacify foreign investors, including those from China:

> ...A government policy of sacrificing labour issues for the sake of attracting foreign investment cannot lead to sustainable development.... The Chinese cannot be blamed for pursuing their objectives.... African trade unions and governments will have to set their own agendas and then *negotiate* the best possible deals with potential investors, including those from China. In the absence of a more *strategic* approach by Africa's political leadership, Chinese investments will be of limited benefit.... (Jauch, 2011: 55, emphasis added)

Take note of the words 'negotiate' and 'strategic'. Let us go back on the premise I begun with by quoting Ha-Joon Chang. It states that FDI should be *strategically* tied to the host nation's developmental requirements and for this to be done states must exercise their bargaining power to *negotiate* good deals for their people instead of acting subservient to non-state actors like MNCs. Specifically this would include things like placing a binding requirement on MNCs to train locals, something that Kohli (2005) argues would have been a wise thing to do for Nigeria.

According to official data, unemployment in Nigeria was 13.4% in 2004, down to 12.3% in 2006, again rising to 14.9% in 2008 and peaking at 21.1% in 2010 (National Bureau of Statistics (NBS), 2010). The rise in redundancy in 2009-10 can however partly be attributed to bleak employment prospects worldwide in the aftermath of the global recession. Although according to some studies Chinese FDI have led to some employment gains in manufacturing and also transfer of skills (Oyeranti, et al., 2010; Haroz, 2011), FDI has clearly not had its overall desired employment generation effects on the Nigerian economy. Neoliberalism has thus ended up escalating existing inequalities by making life worse for the poorer whilst mineral wealth continued to accrue to the elites. The accompanying figure below captures how unemployment shot off the roof in the past decade, coinciding with Nigeria's neoliberal era. Here, mal/non education is seen to be markedly perpetuating class differences.

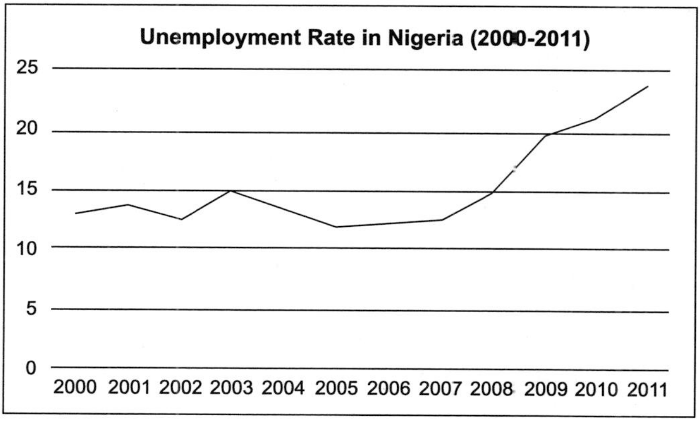

Source: IMF World Economic Outlook, 2014

Upon its own admission, "...years of negligence and adverse policies have led to the underutilization of [existing] resources...human and material.... These resources have not been effectively utilized in order to yield maximum economic benefits. This is one of the primary causes of unemployment and poverty in Nigeria" (NBS, Govt. of Nigeria, 2010: 2). Quite appalling, according to a survey (2010) by NBS, those holding a college degree in fact constitute the greatest number of jobless people, hinting at the poor quality of state sponsored higher education in whatever limited form it exists.[2]

And while natural resources are anyways not the best areas for employment generation and development, FDI in natural resources do not have to be exploitative:

> [...] taking full advantage of the benefits of FDI requires a well educated labour force, to promote technological diffusion and the adoption of better technologies. The same applies to the development of natural resources: here, too, it is beneficial to have a high level of human capital.... It allows for innovation to take place, starting in the natural resources sector and spreading downstream or to other sectors. (Gregorio, 2003: 12)

But, downstream investments which are more productive in terms of employment and technology transfer have hardly seen the light of the day, and in whatever little amount it has, it has not ended in development as corruption and theft mars the sector. As Gillies (2009: 14) points out, "[even] a perfectly managed oil sector will do little to further national development if the resulting revenues are mismanaged or lost due to corruption."

However, the need to diversify one's economy cannot be overstated. And this can be done by way of strategising FDI in the right way. As Lall (2002) points out, two types of FDI strategies are adopted by states—passive and active. An active FDI strategy "involves strong strategic and targeted

2. While the mandate of the book does not cover going into the education and employment scenario in excruciating details, following is a very erudite link to the specific subject of youth unemployment in Nigeria: http://www.brookings.edu/blogs/africa-in-focus/posts/2014/09/23-youth-unemployment-nigeria-akande

interventions by the host government, both to direct FDI in higher value activities and to raise the quality of domestic factors, suppliers and institutes" (*ibid.*: 81). Passive strategies on the other hand have to do with opening up to foreign capital and attracting investors to exploit existing advantages, e.g. natural resources. An active strategy leads to better and greater sharing of FDI benefits and minimises its detrimental effects. By this logic, Nigeria's policy to attract FDI can be only termed as 'extremely passive' to put it gently.

3.2 Trade: Strategies for Development in LDCs

As of today, Nigeria's trade with China stands at $12 bn. This is a mammoth rise from the sum of $330 million that constituted trade between the two countries in 1997. Much attention is now being devoted to the implications for Nigerian development of such a phenomenal deepening of trade relations with China. Aside from the fact that the massive wealth accruing from export of natural resources from Nigeria is diverted by corrupt leaders, the state has also not strategised trade in a manner in which it aids in development. When it adopted an Import Substitution Industrialisation (ISI) regime, it was marred by a wrong set of policies and faulty implementation. I will expand on that in a moment. First, a few facts: Nigeria owes about 50% of its GDP to the oil sector while oil and gas comprises more than 90% of its total export basket (Ogunkola, et al., 2010). This figure is contested by other estimates that peg it around 87%. But while statistical data has never really been either foolproof or objective, the fact of the matter is that the lion's share of Nigeria's exports is comprised by natural resources. This, despite its known expertise in agricultural products. As I will raise later in this section, Nigeria neglected its agricultural exports sector while increasing its dependence on oil exports ever since the commodity started to command high prices during the oil boom.

That said, it is worth pointing out what is one of the most contentious topical issues pertaining to Sino-Nigerian trade: that of Chinese imports into the Nigerian economy allegedly contributing to the obliteration of a domestic industrial base in Nigeria. While one cannot stress enough the futility of reifying unfettered global markets, protectionist policies have done little to help the Nigerian economy either. This is not because a particular policy agenda is not the right (or wrong) thing to follow, but because it is not done the right way. Evans (1995) puts it aptly when he says that what is of significance is not to what extent a state is interventionist or open or should be so, but how it is done.

In a detailed study of the Nigerian state, Biersteker (1987) argues that indigenization has not been panacea to the economic predicaments of Nigeria. Far from it, such policies have only benefited few business elites while welfare concerns of ordinary Nigerians have been abandoned. In fact protection has different effects on different countries and state intervention is not a guaranteed means to development. Nigeria has failed because "...unfortunately for Nigeria, the problems of relative backwardness were compounded by those of an ineffective state" (Kohli, 2005: 363).

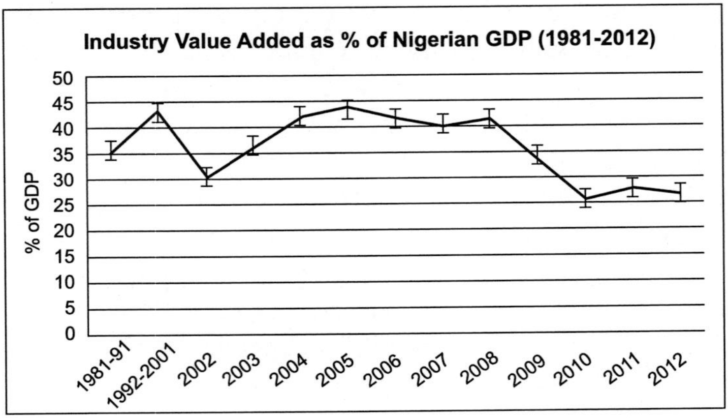

Source: World Development Indicators, various editions (World Bank)

Particularly with respect to protectionist policies in Nigeria, Oyejide et al. (2003) point out how ISI failed in its purpose for want of capable implementation. The authors take the textile sector as a case study and reveal that under an ISI regime the sector actually suffered a decline during which outputs shrank and employment either stagnated or fell. This was much before China kicked off the so-called new scramble for Africa. Therefore when Ayittey talks of Chinese cheap imports bringing down the number of textile factories in Nigeria from five hundred in the eighties to a mere hundred today, he conveniently forgot looking into how the rot started to set in under the ISI regime itself, thanks to a deficient state capacity and policy performance. While the entire logic of ISI was to strengthen domestic industries, the Nigerian state failed to promote indigenous capitalism and manufacturing (Kohli, 2005: 319). Nigerian dependence on import of consumer goods decreased negligibly because home-grown capitalism was still not up to scratch. The failed ISI experience in Africa was clearly due in part to lack of political diligence:

> In the course of import substitution, African countries became less dependent on imported consumer goods, but their dependence on imported intermediate and capital goods increased in the process...East Asian countries that started with import substitution largely avoided these problems by greater discipline within the political class and business community.... (Ake, 1996: 74-75)

Having said that, since neither ISI nor unfettered opening up of markets seem to have worked in Nigeria, it ultimately boils down to the capability of the state in either enforcing protectionist policies as effectively as say South Korea did in its early ISI days, or directing the economy in a manner in which it is then able to cope with international competition.

State power in Nigeria has not just been woefully underused (by allowing FDI a free reign, etc.), but misdirected and misused (neopatrimonialism, corruption, etc.), and in some cases, inefficiently used (as the textile example and many others demonstrate).

The statistical tabulation below by way of a table and a graph reveals that industries' share of the GDP went down every passing decade. In fact, the accompanying graph indicates big ups and downs throughout the course of three decades up to 2012, and in fact a sharp downward trend in the last few years. Data also seems to point out that the share of industries in GDP was the highest in the decade, 1991-2000 (43.66%) as against 34.76% during the heydays of ISI in Nigeria. The argument that opening up the economy have had cascading effects on the economy to the point of de-industrialising the same, again, does not quite hold up in the face of the following data which shows the 2001-05 average of 38.75% is comfortably higher than the 1981-90 average of industries' share of GDP. At the heart of the problem really was the failure of the state, and we keep discussing on those lines, including venturing into the agricultural sector debate.

Share of Industries Value Added as a % of GDP in Nigeria (1981-2012)

1981	39.96
1982	35.45
1983	30.87
1984	28.33
1985	29.86
1986	27.16
1987	35.30
1988	31.79
1989	43.60
1990	45.27
1981-90	**34.76**

(*Contd...*)

1991	45.76
1992	53.00
1993	42.69
1994	32.86
1995	46.02
1996	48.52
1997	44.14
1998	33.56
1999	37.86
2000	52.21
1991-2000	**43.66**
2001	40.87
2002	30.52
2003	36.75
2004	42.09
2005	43.51
2001-05	**38.75**
2006	41.92
2007	40.65
2008	41.48
2009	34.21
2010	25.81
2011	27.85
2012	26.72
2006-12	**34.09**

One is also forced to ask as to why Nigeria with all its primary goods possessions did not manage to reap its full benefits through trade? Actually, Nigeria's gradual moving away from agricultural exports was justified by technocrats who believed development entails an exclusive focus on manufactured goods. It also had to do with increasing discovery of oil, which I come to next. While ISI was meant to create an indigenous manufacturing base, (setting the stage perhaps for export of manufactures) it did not succeed. In fact, Kaplinsky (2003), working under the Global Commodity Chain (GCC) framework, questions the very conventional policy prescription of having to move away from trading in agricultural goods to manufactures in order to develop, and argues that LDCs and developing countries, especially in sub-Saharan Africa, need to combat declining terms of trade and this can be done without abandoning agriculture. The crux of the statement is that while industrialisation needs pursuance, agricultural commodities can contribute to development. While world-system theorists rake up the structural imbalances in international trade, the GCC framework, ironically inflected by WST, seeks to convert this into an opportunity for development. Upgrading under the GCC framework is done in three forms or stages: process upgrading where firms produce more efficiently; product upgrading where quality of products are boosted; and functional upgrading which concerns itself with moving up the value chain itself, for instance engaging in packaging and branding. However, these would require local institutions and a national strategic focus on 'factor creating mechanisms' like public investments that enable countries to complement their natural factor endowments (Porter, 1998).

While Ghana is not separate from the continental malaise of Africa, it has demonstrated that developmental gains can be made even with agricultural exports—that is, if the state plays its role adeptly. Having been subject to a colonial experience no different from Nigeria, Ghana too was a non-industrialised geographical expanse, managing to scrape through as a nation by exporting agricultural goods when it started out. However, soon it started to make use of trade for its own development. Using a 'staple theory of growth' framework, Boame (1998) documents how Ghana gradually developed backward, forward and 'final-demand' linkages through its export of cocoa. Backward linkages included the setting up of improved physical infrastructure by the state in response to the expanding export sector. Forward linkages were the "...most important in the further processing of the output from the export sector...[as] the processed exports increase the value added...in foreign markets" (*ibid.*: 177). Thus institutions can aid functional upgrading, which can then lead to development of communities. Nigeria has no such demonstrable upgrading experience in its huge cashew industry, thanks to a state which has not just failed in the governance of natural resources, but in its obsession with organised corruption in the sector, has hardly ever managed to look beyond the oil sector ever since it started to dominate its export basket during the oil boom of the 70s, before which primary exports mostly included agricultural products like cashew, cocoa, groundnuts, etc. Also, whereas export revenue (from minerals and agricultural products) in Ghana was used to finance education and health, the revenues that accrued to the Nigerian state through its mineral and agricultural exports led to something quite different. As a commentator on the Nigerian state put it:

> In Nigeria, the wealth derived from oil resource exploitation and exports benefit directly only the operators of the oil industry and the bureaucrats in government. (Celestine, 2003: 34)

The following table and figure attest to the poor attention that the Nigerian state bestowed on health, for example. There's a massive blip in public health spending in the beginning of the century, while taking off thereafter, only to fall further ahead. Overall, there's actually a declining trend in health sector expenditure.

Public Health Expenditure as a % of GDP in Nigeria (1995-2012)

1995	8.429481
1996	8.429481
1997	8.429481
1998	8.429481
1999	5.528497
2000	4.219594
2001	3.201079
2002	3.246251
2003	4.78771
2004	8.360212
2005	8.258012
2006	8.296944
2007	9.390997
2008	9.237138
2009	7.869831
2010	5.496342
2011	6.660911
2012	6.660911

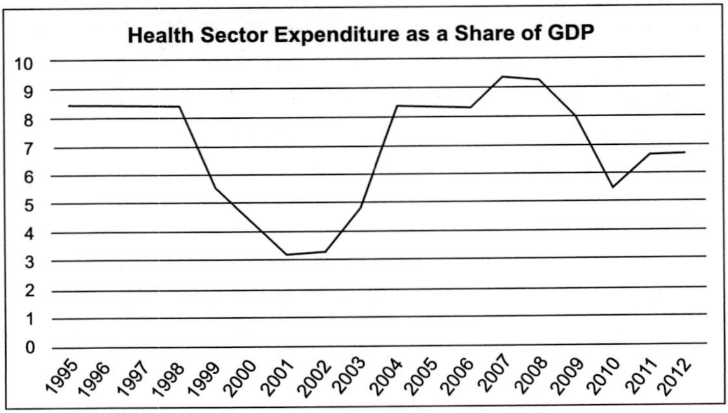

Source: World Development Indicators, various editions (World Bank)

Mitchell (2009) rightfully claims that revenues from mineral exports should ideally be used to finance social welfare. Perhaps Ghana's relatively successful run has a lot to do with the fact that it is one of the least corrupt states in Africa (Transparency International, 2011), as much as Nigeria's failure has to do with the fact that it is an epitome of institutional corruption. The following table/graph reveals how oil rents continued to dominate the economy throughout Nigeria's history of independent existence.

Oil Obsession Persists

	Oil rents as % of GDP
1970-78	18.32
1979-87	36.16
1988-96	38.78
1997-2005	32.2
2006	33.25
2007	29.55
2008	31.13
2009	22.42
2010	25.02
2011	30.21
2012	26.80

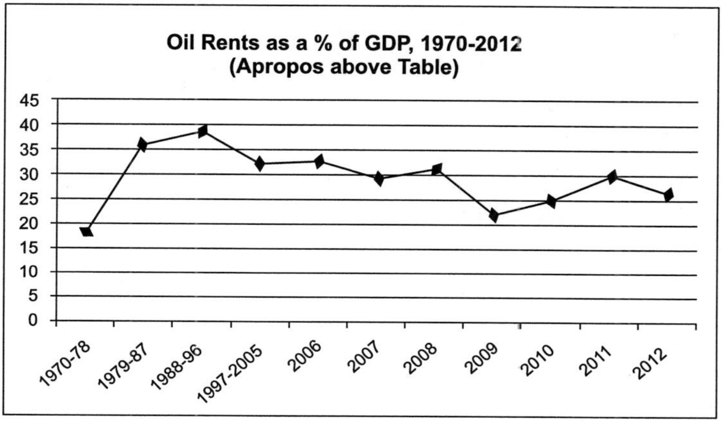

The period 1988-96 was the most notorious, data reveals. While, agriculture faced the abandon and oil kept lining the pockets of the elite, Nigeria continued to suffer on almost all economic and social counts.

In the following section where I discuss the much-touted probability of Chinese neo-colonialism in Nigeria, I factor in the element of institutionalised corruption in the host country, a correlation which has so far attracted less attention.

3.3 Chinese Neoimperialism and the Nigerian State

For its critiques, neoliberalism "...appears as the most recent in the longer tradition of imperialism" (Harrison, 2010: 22). And neoliberal globalisation in sub-Saharan Africa has seemingly taken an imperialist form. According to Hahn (2008), neoliberalism cannot be analysed without its links to neo-colonialism duly explored. In line with the above premise, the spectre of Chinese capital in Nigeria—and indeed the whole of Africa—is considered to be an attempt at neo-colonialism by China (Ogen, 2008, Sanusi, 2013, among others). Some have also suggested, rather contradictorily, that China-Nigeria ties represent both South-South solidarity and neo-colonialism at the same time (Wagner and Cafiero, 2013). But quite aside from the fact that most of the neo-colonialism charge runs deep in Western academic circles giving scholars like Mohan (2009) reason to doubt the knowledge production in the first place, it is imperative to bring the host state into any analysis on imperialism. This calls for an understanding of the 'African state' as it were. With that I will also talk about corrupt political institutions and patrimonial leaders in Nigeria in the context of it being allegedly subject to neoimperialism.

It is in the middle of Nigeria's steadfast promotion of neoliberalism, having marched past the ISI days, that Rene N'Guetta Kouassi, the head of the African Union's economic affairs department, warned that "Africa must not jump blindly from one type of neo-colonialism into Chinese-style neo-colonialism" (Agence France-Presse, Sept. 30, 2009). He was only adding to the long list of similar charges. But neo-imperialism in Africa must be seen as a function of the host state wherein the state has been unable to carry out its task as the upholder of the rights of its citizens while being hand in gloves with foreign capital behind the scenes, thus divesting foreign capital of its beneficial impacts and reducing it to an imperial partner, eventually making it the subject of much popular aversion.

The contemporary demonization of Chinese FDI in Nigeria is a direct descendent of the historical indictment of foreign capital because of the claim that foreign economic and political dominance have foiled the establishment of a domestic manufacturing industry and indigenous trading houses despite the presence of large domestic markets like Nigeria. Kasfir calls these elements the "colonial monopolists" who blocked the advance of indigenous capitalism. But in a post-colonial state, monopoly is only possible when the state does not lay down fair and transparent rules and instead has a vested interest in the business activities of foreign companies. This brings us back to Ake (1996) who talks about "a predatory state and politics [that] have ruined the prospects for development by spreading...inefficiency and corruption" (p. 117). State-business relations in the state crudely border on the illicit, informal and undemocratic (Taylor, 1996). In fact often members of the ruling class acting as middlemen are so deeply engaged in enabling foreign capital's penetration so as to derail a transparent allocation of resources. Frynas (1998) goes on to conduct a case study of the oil MNC Shell and divulges alarming details of its business activities which lay bare the sheer lack of transparency and fairness:

> Nigeria had the advantage for Shell because it had ready oil reserves for unlimited depletion, the country's rulers were willing to rely heavily on oil.... Shell has many formal and informal agreements with state agencies that range from questions of land acquisition to the purchase of arms for the police.... Shell has built up a network of personal contacts in Nigeria. (*ibid.*: 472-73)

Just as the Shell example highlighted by Frynas shows, the state itself is a party to, if not the architect of exploitative FDI activities. Theoretically, this warrants a study of imperialism that is not disproportionately focused on the role of foreign capital while neglecting that of the host state's:

> The empirical study of imperialism in the third world today should therefore be the study of the manner in which *state power* is used to protect the monopoly interests of international capital. The relationship between imperialism and 'underdevelopment' is therefore the extent to which such state protection holds back the development of the productive forces. (Beckman, 1981: 18, emphasis added)

If monopolistic conditions are granted to foreign capital in a sovereign country they only speak of vested interests in the domestic political elite, whereas the right institutional circumstance would guarantee better ground rules for competitive capitalism, thus unshackling productivity. This harks back to the three crucial points I had earlier made: that *state power* in Nigeria has been underused, misused and inefficiently used with alternating frequency, thus never managing to pull the masses out of poverty and deprivation.

What's more, corruption is no longer a case of few (or many) stray elements in the government and bureaucracy; it is formal, institutionalised and systemic. Bayart, et al. (1999) calls this the 'criminalisation of the state' and see this as constituting the privatization of state institutions and the development of "economies of plunder" through state-supported criminal activities mainly in the resources sector. In fact the entire "politics in Africa is becoming markedly interconnected with crime" (*ibid.*: 25). The "moi je m'enfou" (translation: I don't give a damn) attitude that underpins the lack of accountability in the state, egged on by a society that is undemocratic enough not to be able to challenge such practices, end up chiefly contributing to endemic poverty in independent Africa (*ibid.*).

Corruption as having acted as a barrier to economic growth and development in sub-Saharan Africa is a stance taken by many commentators. But the issue of suspected neo-colonialism in Nigeria has seldom been inquired into by correlating it with host country corruption. When no less than the outgoing Nigerian central bank governor was giving out warning signals of a neo-colonial invasion by China (*Financial Times*, 2013), it might be assumed that he was by implication charging the Nigerian state institutions of silent participation. Because while corruption can be indeed be sourced to colonialism, sovereign Nigeria had the chance to choose to be non-corrupt:

> ...if self-determination gave African leaders the opportunity to choose what was good for their people, then one would be justified in arguing that the opportunity has existed for them to choose non-corrupt practices. That they did not opt for that path is a clear indication of the total lack of commitment and political will by the continent's political and bureaucratic elites to depart from corruption. (Mulinge and Lesetedi, 1998: 25)

Taking forward from the authors' synthesis, I put it that while colonialism had led to the establishment and evolution of corrupt institutions, persistence of extractive institutions in the post-colonial state is a sign that the state is both incompetent and often a comprador. In that sense the Nigerian political elite invites and potentially begets neo-colonialism by international capital. Nigeria's *Vanguard* newspaper in fact alleges that corrupt elitism (or elite corruption?) also occurs at the sub-national level wherein, "small circle of elites retain huge resources using strong arm tactics of all types."[3]

Since 1999 when after years of military rule Nigeria adopted its fourth republic constitution and apparently returned to a democratic political system (though a far cry from genuine democracy), Nigeria has gone through what Ingwe, et al. (2012) effectively identifies as plunder in the name of neoliberalism. The authors go on to say that the elite establishment methodically rendered the opponents of the corrupt neoliberalistic formations impotent. On the lack of vibrancy in the economy and social justice, the authors mention that the underfunding of universities led to the "weakening of vibrant independent scholarship" (*ibid.*: 34) and a deliberate discouragement of domestic entrepreneurship.

With regards to allegations that Chinese investments are planting the seeds of neo-colonialism in Africa, it is worth mentioning then that the 'FDI-amounts-to-resource-imperialism' contention is quite simply untrue. Well-managed natural resource endowments have no reason to not aid in sustained growth, provided institutions stand for good

3. To know more about the current/topical state of corruption in Nigeria, consider reading the following media coverage of the issue:

   Link 1: http://www.dailymail.co.uk/debate/article-2387359/Nigeria-country-corrupt-better-burn-aid-money.html

   Link 2: http://www.theguardian.com/global-development/poverty-matters/2014/jul/11/boko-haram-nigeria-violence-corruption-security

   Link 3: http://allafrica.com/stories/200712190147.html (needs subscription to access full article)

governance and transparency, not exploitation. Examples of well managed resources contributing to development include Chile's copper, Botswana's diamond and Indonesia's oil. In the table below, I pit sets of statistical data against each other in a bid to capture state failure in its entirety. It reflects the whole range of ineptitude, right from the state's apathetic response to the basic infrastructural needs of the country, to the developmental cost of its institutional corruption, to its inability to strategise trade for development.

Table 1: Oil Wealth, Corruption, Neglect of Agriculture and Slack Infrastructure in Nigeria

Government revenue through mineral export earnings (2006-10)	Estimated investment required in setting up basic physical infrastructure	% share of manufacturing in GDP	Estimated money lost to corruption (2000-10)	Estimated govt revenue usurped by SaniAbacha alone	Potential for cashew and shea butter exports
$50bn/year (Average)	$19bn/year	4.1% only (FY 2011)	$3.5bn/ year	$50bn (1993-97)	$3.5bn/year (Combined)

Sources: Olomola (2007), Nigerian Federal Ministry of Petroleum Resources, National Planning Commission of Nigeria, OPEC, Bloomberg, Manufacturers Association of Nigeria, National Cashew Association of Nigeria

4

Conclusion

According to Nigeria's National Bureau of Statistics, 60.9% of Nigerians in 2010 were living in "absolute poverty"—rising from 54.7% in 2004. This was also the time when Chinese FDI in Nigeria grew rapidly and GDP growth in Nigeria was sustained at roughly around 5-8%. Despite growth, Nigerian people continue to reel under poverty and unemployment is hardly heading off. However, this automatically does *not* lead to the conclusion that Chinese FDI or for that matter any FDI is essentially meant to wreck havoc in the Nigerian economy or contribute to Nigerian impoverishment. This paper has conceptualised poverty in Nigeria through the analytical lens of the state, which is known to be a historically shaped social institution.

I have argued that FDI in developing countries including in the natural resources sector can indeed be of benefit and it is the host state that needs to ensure that FDI works to its benefit. An active FDI policy would also attract investments in more productive sectors of the economy with an eye on social development. It is clear that 'getting institutions right' is a recipe for development. If the state is corrupt and careless about the needs of the masses (like the

Nigerian state is), one does need to look outside to find an answer to underdevelopment—it lies within. To understand underdevelopment, poverty is often taken as an endpoint which then is sought to be accounted for. However, if one were to instead take Nigerian underdevelopment as the starting point of analysis and seek to not just explain the wretchedness, but look for what might help coming out of poverty, the strength of dependency theories will be limited to a considerable extent. To be sure, the vicious cycle of poverty can be ended. But that will warrant neither an adherence to free markets nor turning to socialism. Development will essentially require better institutional setting—in the Nigerian case this would mean reforming the politics of the state towards a democratic setup, limiting corruption, developing better basic infrastructure and a reasonably virtuous workforce supported by the state, for starters. It can be followed by welfare spending and appropriate legislative reforms. More specifically what is needed is a combination of fair and transparent bidding of natural resources and an active FDI strategy that links foreign capital with domestic developmental needs:

> In Nigeria, a lack of strong institutions has led to constrained progress in [the] areas of infrastructure, agriculture, and technology transfer. Similarly, widespread corruption has not transferred wealth to the lower classes...Nigeria [has to] develop credible, accountable, and transparent institutions. (Nabine, 2009: 21)

Espousing the fact that an effective and strong state is a means to development is nothing like believing in some abstract neo-classical arithmetic as if it were engineering. The veneration of institutions and the highlighting of the role of the state are rooted in, and enthused by, some real material developmental experiences of the contemporary world. It is worth concluding by recapping that neoliberal globalisation, characterised by transnational movement of capital and goods, is not a force potent enough to trample over states; it is merely reflective of a contemporary global political economy that needs shrewd *managing* by sovereign territories like Nigeria in order to *exploit* the same for its own developmental aspirations. As Newell (2002) asserts, the extent to which globalisation helps the poor is a product of institutional design and political organisation. Finally, a clarification: it has not for a moment been the intention of this paper to let Chinese capital off the hook, but simply to bring the host state back into the analysis. After all, MNCs are merely answerable to its limited number of shareholders; a state has a social contract to fulfil and is answerable to its citizens—in this case, 163 million Nigerians.

Bibliography

African Development Bank Group (2009), "Nigeria economic and power sector reform program (EPSERP) Appraisal Report". August, 2009, Available at: <http://www.afdb.org/>

Ake, C. (1996), *Democracy and Development in Africa*, Brookings Institution, Washington DC.

Al-Sadig, A. (2012), "The effects of foreign direct investment on private domestic investment: evidence from developing countries", *Empirical Economics*, Vol. 44, Issue 3, pp. 1267-75.

Amin, S. (1990), *Maldevelopment: Anatomy of a Global Failure*, London: Zed Books.

Amsden, A.H. (1989), *Asia's Next Giant: South Korea and Late Industrialization*, Oxford: Oxford University Press.

Anele, D. (2013), "The Spiritual Poverty of Nigeria's Ruling Elite", *Vanguard*, June 23, Available at: <http://www.vanguardngr.com/2013/06/the-spiritual-poverty-of-nigerias-ruling-elite/>

Arrighi, G. (2007), *Adam Smith in Beijing: Lineages of the Twenty-First Century*, London: Verso.

Ayanwale, A.B. (2007), "FDI and Economic Growth: Evidence from Nigeria", AERC Research Paper 165, African Economic Research Consortium, Nairobi, April 2007.

Bayart, J.F., Ellis, S. and Hibou, B. (1999), *The Criminalization of the State in Africa,* Oxford: James Currey.

Beckman, B. (1981), "Imperialism and the 'National Bourgeoisie'", *Review of African Political Economy*, No. 22 (Oct. - Dec., 1981), pp. 5-19.

Biersteker, T.J. (1987), *Multinationals, the State and Control of the Nigerian Economy*, Princeton: Princeton University Press.

Braunstein, E. and Epstein, G. (2002), "Bargaining Power and Foreign Direct Investment in China: Can 1.3 Billion Consumers Tame the Multinationals?" in *Labour and the Globalization of Production*, William Milberg, Ed. London: Palgrave Macmillan.

Celestine, A. (2003), "Hydrocarbon Exploitation, Environmental Degradation and Poverty: The Niger Delta Experience", Kairus Consulting Limited, Lagos, Nigeria, 2003, pp. 32-37.

Chang, H.J. (1998), "Globalization, transnational corporation, and economic development: can the developing countries pursue strategic industrial policy in a globalizing world economy?" in Baker, D., Epstein, G. and Pollin, R. (eds.), *Globalization and Progressive Economic Policy,* Cambridge University Press, pp. 97-113.

Collier, P. (2010), "The Political Economy of Natural Resources", *Social Research,* Vol. 77, No. 4, pp. 1105-32.

Daniel, P. (1991), "Foreign Investment Revisited", *IDS Bulletin*, Vol. 22, No. 2, *Institute of Development Studies*, Brighton, 1991.

Dinda, S. (2008), "Factors Determining FDI to Nigeria: An Empirical Investigation", MPRA Paper No. 40170, Available at <http://mpra.ub.uni-muenchen.de/40170/> Accessed: 18 Jun. 2013.

Erunke, C.E. and Kigbu, H. (2012), "Globalization, Multinational Corporation and the Nigerian Economy", *International Journal of Social Science Tomorrow*, Vol. 1, No. 2, pp. 1-8.

Evans, P. (1995), *Embedded Autonomy: States and Industrial Transformation,* Princeton, NJ: Princeton University Press.

Federal Ministry of Petroleum Resources (2012), "Report of the Petroleum Revenue Special Task Force", August, 2012. Individually unverified copy available at: <http://www.saharareporters.com/> Accessed on: 26 August, 2013.

Ficker, S.K. (2005), "From Structuralism to the New Institutional Economics", *Latin American Research Review,* Vol. 40, No. 3, pp. 145-62.

Frank, A.G. (1972), "Economic Dependence, Class Structure and Underdevelopment Policy", in Cockcroft, J.D., Frank, A.G. and Johnson, D.L. (eds.), *Dependence and Underdevelopment: Latin America's Political Economy*, pp. 19-46. Garden City, N.Y.: Anchor Books.

Frynas, J.G. (1998), "Political Instability and Business: Focus on Shell in Nigeria", *Third World Quarterly*, Vol. 19, No. 3, pp. 457-78.

Gillies, A. (2009), "Reforming corruption out of Nigerian oil?", U4 Anti-Corruption Resource Center Brief, No. 2, Chr. Michelsen Institute, Bergen. Available at: <http://www.cmi.no/publications/>

Graham, Edward M. (2000), "Globalization, Foreign Direct Investment and Labour", *Fighting the Wrong Enemy:*

Antiglobal Activists and Multilateral Enterprises, Peterson Institute, pp. 81-130.

Gregorio, J.D. (2003), "The Role of Foreign Direct Investment and Natural Resources in Economic Development", Central Bank of Chile Working Paper, No. 196, Available at: <http://www.bcentral.cl/eng/studies/working-papers/>

Hahn, N.S.C. (2008), "Neoliberal Imperialism and Pan-African Resistance", *Journal of World-Systems Research*, Vol. XIII, No. 2, pp. 142-78.

Hariss, J., Hunter, J. and Lewis, C.M. (1995), "Development and Significance of NIE", in Hariss, J. et al. (eds.), *The New Institutional Economics and Third World Development,* Routledge, pp. 1-16.

Haroz, D. (2011), "China in Africa: Symbiosis or Exploitation?" *The Fletcher Forum of World Affairs*, May, 2011, Available at: <http://www.fletcherforum.org/2011/05/15/haroz/>

Jauch, H. (2011), "Chinese Investments in Africa: Twenty-First Century Colonialism?" *New Labor Forum*, Vol. 20, Issue 2, pp. 48-55.

Kaplinsky, R. (2003), "How can agricultural commodity producers appropriate a greater share of value chain outcomes?", Institute of Development Studies, University of Sussex & Center for Research in Innovation Management, University of Brighton.

Kasfir, N. (1983), "Relating Class to State in Africa", *The Journal of Commonwealth & Comparative Politics*, Vol. 21, No. 3, pp. 1-20.

Kohli, A. (2005), *State-directed Development*, Cambridge: Cambridge University Press.

Kousari, K. (2005), "Africa's Development and External Constraints", in Teunissen, J.J. and Akkerman, A. (eds.), *Africa in the World Economy—The National, Regional and International Challenges*, Fondad, The Hague, pp. 169-85.

Lall, S. (2002), "Transnational Corporations and Technology Flows", in Nayyar, D. (ed.), *Governing Globalisation: Issues and Institutions,* Oxford University Press, pp. 78-107.

Levitt, K.P. (2006), "Keynes and Polanyi: The 1920s and the 1990s" *Review of International Political Economy*, Vol. 13, No. 1, pp. 152-77.

Lewis, P.M. (2006), "The Dysfunctional State of Nigeria" in Birdsall, N., Vaishnav, M. and Ayres, R.L. (eds.), *Short of the Goal*, Brookings Institution Press, pp. 83-116.

Manufacturers Association of Nigeria (2011), "39th Annual General Meeting Report", 12 Sept. 2011, Available at: <http://www.manufacturersnigeria.org/>. Accessed on: 10 Aug. 2013.

Maswana, J.C. (2007), "China-Africa's Emerging Economic Links: A Review under the Core-Periphery Perspective", in *The Annual Conference of World Association for the Political Economy* (WAPE), Oct. 27-28, Shimane, Japan.

Mehlum, H., Moene, K. and Torvik, R. (2002), "Institutions and the Resource Curse", University of Oslo, Memo Series No. 29. Oct, 2002.

Meyersson, E., Miquel, G.P. and Quian, N. (2008), "The Rise of China and the Natural Resource Curse in Africa", EOPP Research series, London School of Economics, Available at: <http://sticerd.lse.ac.uk/eopp/new/research/>

Mohan, G. and Lampert, B. (2013), "Negotiating China: Reinserting African Agency into China-Africa Relations", *African Affairs*, Vol. 112, No. 446, pp. 92-110.

Moran, T.H. (2006), "Toward Best Outcomes from Foreign Direct Investment in Poorly Performing States" in Birdsall, N., et al. (eds.), *Short of the Goal*, Brookings Institution Press, pp. 334-75.

Mulinge, M.M. and Lesetedi, G.N. (1998), "Interrogating Our Past: Colonialism and Corruption in Sub-Saharan Africa", *African Journal of Political Science*, Vol. 3, No. 2, pp. 15-28.

Nabine, D.W. (2009), "The Impact of Chinese Investment and Trade on Nigeria Economic Growth", African Trade Policy Center Working Paper No. 77, Shanghai, Available at: <http://www.uneca.org>

National Bureau of Labour Statistics, Nigeria (2010), "National Manpower Stock and Employment Generation Survey", July, 2010, Available at: <http://nigerianstat.gov.ng>

National Cashew Association of Nigeria (2012), Interview by Layi Adeloye, "Nigerian cashew industry loses N177bn annually", Punch Nigeria Limited, Feb 8. Available at: <http://www.punchng.com/business/business-economy/nigerian-cashew-industry-loses-n177bn-annually/>

Newell, P. (2002), "Globalisation and the Future State", IDS Working Paper 141, Institute of Development Studies, Brighton, April 2002, Available at: <http://www.ids.ac.uk/>

Ogen, O. (2008), "Contemporary China-Nigeria Economic Relations: Chinese Imperialism or South-South Mutual Partnership?" *China aktuell-Journal of Current Chinese Affairs,* Vol. 37, No. 3, 2008, pp. 78-102.

Oliveira, R.S.D. (2008), "Making sense of Chinese oil investment in Africa", in Alden, C., Large, D. and Oliveira, R.S.D. (eds.), *China Returns to Africa: A*

Rising Power and a Continent Embrace, New York: Columbia University Press, pp. 83-110.

Oyejide, T.A., Ogunkola, E.O., Jerome, A., Adenikinju, A. and Bankole, A.S. (2003), "The Impact of Trade Liberalization on Nigeria's Textile Sector", Abuja: Report for the World Bank.

Oyeranti, O.A., Babatunde, M.A., Ogunkola, E.O. and Bankole, A.S. (2010), "China Africa Investment Relations: A Case Study of Nigeria", African Economic Research Consortium, Nairobi, Kenya, 2010.

Ozughalu, U.M. and Ogwumike, F.O. (2013), "Can Economic Growth, Foreign Direct Investment And Exports Provide The Desired Panacea To The Problem Of Unemployment In Nigeria?", *Journal of Economics and Sustainable Development*, Vol. 4, No. 1, pp. 36-51.

Rama, M. (2002), "Globalization and Workers in Developing Countries", (Economics Series Working Paper No. 41), East West Center, Hawaii, Available from: <http://www.eastwestcenter.org/publications/browse-all-series/east-west-center-working-papers-economics-series>

Roychowdhury, S. (2004), "Globalisation and Labour", *Economic and Political Weekly*, Vol. 39, No, 1, pp. 105-08.

Sanusi, L. (2013), "Africa must get real about Chinese ties", *Financial Times,* 11 March, Available at: <http://www.ft.com/cms/s/0/562692b0-898c-11e2-ad3f-00144feabdc0.html>

Sen, A. (2013), Interview by Sagarika Ghose. *Face the People*. CNN-IBN, New Delhi: 21 July, 2013. Television.

Sklair, L. (2001), *The Transnational Capitalist Class*, Oxford: Blackwell.

Stiglitz, J. (2012), "Africa's natural resources can be a blessing, not an economic curse", *The Guardian*, 6 Aug, Available at: <http://www.theguardian.com/business/economics-blog/2012/aug/06/africa-natural-resources-economic-curse>

Taylor, S.D. (2007), *Business and the State in Southern Africa: The Politics of Economic Reform*, London: Lynne Rienner.

Transparency International (2011), "Overview of Corruption and Anti-corruption in Ghana", Available at: <http://www.u4.no/publications/overview-of-corruption-and-anti-corruption-in-ghana/> Accessed on: 26 Aug. 2013.

Turner, T. (1976), "Multinational Corporations and the Instability of the Nigerian State", *Review of African Political Economy*, Vol. 3, No. 5, pp. 63-79.

Vanguard (2013), "2013 Budget: Rescuing Education", Nov. 26, 2012. Available at: <http://www.vanguardngr.com/2012/11/2013-budget-rescuing-education/>. Accessed on: 26 Aug. 2013.